Fishy Listing, Just Surfaced!

Original Redwood Interior!

Open Floor Plan!

Ocean Front Property

Champagne Living on a Beer Budget!

REAL ESTATE BARGAINS!

REAL ESTATE BARGAINS!

Homes You Can Afford . . . But May Not Want

BY MARTIN PETER PORISS

BEST GIFT PRESS
SANTA CRUZ, CA

A Parody This book is a spoof, nothing but a spoof, and it's intended to be only a spoof. No property featured herein is actually for sale. Rather, all materials herein are simply the author's interpretation of photographs and language. No aspersions are meant to any properties or people pictured herein; no aspersions are meant to any persons, real or imagined, living or dead; and no aspersions are meant to any companies or corporations, real or imagined.

Copyright © 1989, 2000 by Martin Peter Poriss (aka Peter Martin)
The next to last page of this book constitutes a continuation of this copyright page.
2000 edition has been completely revised.

All Rights Reserved Worldwide. Reproduction or transmittal or use of this book, in whole or in part, in any manner or in any form whatsoever, by any means, electronic or photographic or mechanical, including photocopying, recording or by any information storage and retrieval system, except by a reviewer for the inclusion of brief quotations and no more than two photographs in a published review, is strictly prohibited. All rights, including the right of translation into other languages, are fully reserved under the International Copyright Union, the Universal Copyright Convention and the Pan American Copyright Convention.

Rip-Off Artists Beware! Best Gift Press rewards whistle-blowers! Two hundred fifty dollars ($250)—plus 10% of all monies received from any legal action—will be awarded to the first person who sends the publisher a sample of the unauthorized use of any materials from this book (by an individual or company) for marketing or for any other commercial purposes, which use constitutes a copyright violation. The identity of the sender will be kept confidential. For complete information regarding the conditions for earning this award, please visit www.RealEstateThings.com.

Published by:
Real Estate Bargains has been published as a joint effort between Century Publishing Company, Inc., and Best Gift Press, an imprint of the Martin Company, LLC. Century Publishing is the nation's largest publisher of customized real estate magazines for individual agents and offices.

This edition is an expansion and revision of a work by the same title, previously published by Peters Press copyright © 1989 by Peter Martin (aka Martin Peter Poriss)
Printed and bound in the U.S.A. by Century Publishing Company, Inc., Coeur d'Alene, Idaho

ISBN: 0-9668110-0-3
Library of Congress Catalog Card Number available

ATTENTION REAL ESTATE AGENTS AND MORTGAGE BROKERS: For gift giving and other purposes, quantity discounts are available on bulk purchases of ten or more (10+) copies of this book.

Visit us at www.RealEstateThings.com

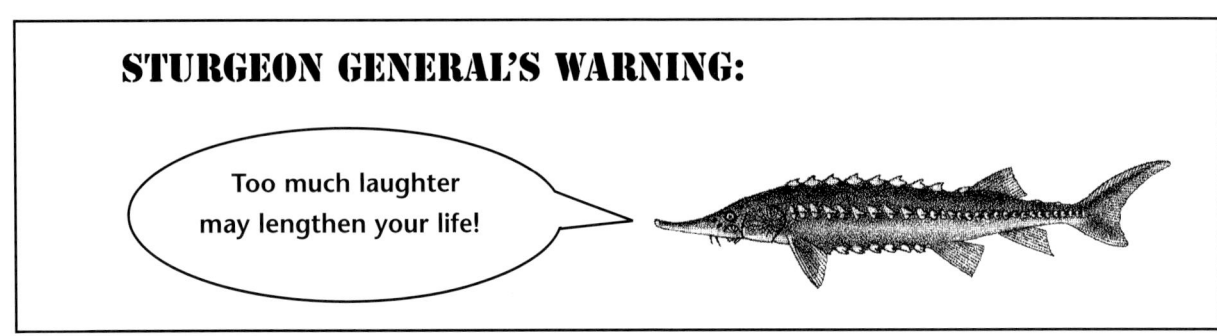

Absolutely No Fakes!

Like the "eggstatic image" to the right, the photograph on the front cover of this book is of a real building. The photo was *not* diddled with in a darkroom, nor was it "enhanced" on a computer. It does *not* consist of more than one image; nor was it morphed, retouched, tweaked by digital manipulation, or the result of the author having accidentally dripped coffee or strawberry jam onto the negative. Rather, the building featured on the cover was built just as it appears in the photograph. (Notice the entrance between the peaks of the roof…and the floor running across the inside of the bottom right front window.)

In fact, absolutely none of the photographs in this book were produced by "trick photography"…nor were any of them changed by computer "enhancement." On the contrary: all of the buildings in this book are entirely real! They (and everything in, on, and around them) were photographed in their natural habitats, precisely as you see them here, in *Real Estate Bargains!*

For My Mom . . .
Who, for nine months, provided me with my first
rather comfortable, albeit tiny, "starter home"

Has a small lien on it...

Ocean View Property!

PHOTO BY ALLEN GRASSO

Wave-of-the-Future Living! Enjoy sweeping, stunning, unobstructed ocean views. Pickled oak cabinets, whitewashed beams, bay windows. Exceptionally clean! Imagine the fun . . . as you experience eye-popping views of the coast from this exciting home. Don't delay. See this seaside home today!

Located in East Bovine

Crème de la Crème!

In the mooood for a fixer-upper? Like the cows, this home is out standing in its field. Udderly pastoral! Own this home and milk the property for all it's worth!

Open Floor Plan!

Reduced to Sell! Make indoor-outdoor living yours in this well-ventilated home. Exceptional master bedroom suite boasts a well-lit bath with large mirror. *(Note the photographer shooting himself in the mirror!)* In this elegant chamber, you'll feel flushed with pride, as you realize that (almost) all is vanity. Central air. Central vacuum. Washer-dryer remaining.

Douglas Fir Interior!

Split Level Home . . .
Woodsy feeling throughout.
Free firewood included!

Don't let this one slip by! Two partial homes for the price of one. Excellent hillside views! Possible lot split. Great yard for kids. Owner anxious.

Commuter's Dream! Easy freeway access, along with an unusual view. Look down upon a fast-moving, year-round stream! Never boring. *A large home, for those who like to live life in the fast lane.*

Floating Mortgage Rate!

Pier Pressure! Fish from your very own living room, while you tide yourself over with this charming houseboat. Some say you'd have to be a little dinghy to live here, but this cozy retreat offers easy maintenance . . . since the landscaping never needs to be watered.

A Very Mobile Home!

Buoy, Oh Buoy! This multi-level complex allows you to sea forever and beyond. These adjacent boat-homes are served, paradoxically, by a pair of docks. A thought-provoking set of homes, *and a great deal to sink about!*

Seller to leave houseplants and skylight…

Small but cozy . . . "Built like a brick s✶✶t-house," according to the editors of *Architectural Digestion*. Simple floor plan is quaint and charming. A wonderful rural get-away for families with little furniture.

PHOTO BY CARL VITI/HONOLULU ADVERTISER

New Subdivision! Just broke ground . . . so scramble on over to select your new home. Merely a stone's throw from schools and shopping. Perfect for those who enjoy all-terrain recreational vehicles!

Special Exterior Siding!

Hottest Deal of the Month: Charcoal gray in color. Easily located by your friends, visitors, and old flames. Built by the Coleman family. Later served as a rehearsal studio for the *Briquettes,* a group that made famous the old standby, *When Smoke Gets in Your Eyes.*

Focus On this One!

Attention bird watchers, voyeurs and far-sighted visionaries: this property lens itself to many possibilities. Provides tremendous views. Call *Seymour Real Estate!*

www.RealEstateThings.com

A Real Cream Puff . . . or Five?!

Especially suited to well-rounded individuals. Architectural styling evokes a feeling of refined simplicity and understated elegance. First time on market in over 900 years. Original owner. A rare purchasing opportunity in Beautiful Downtown Bedrock. Call *B.C. Realty* . . . and ask for Fred or Wilma.

Canoe Afford This One?

Riverview Property . . . Back to nature! Let the sweet sounds of a nearby babbling stream lull you to sleep. Basement swimming pool. Security moat. Wet bar. Cost effective landscape irrigation system. Convenient for boating enthusiasts. Won't last long.

New Roe House, Just Surfaced!
Probably a large school nearby. Feel lured?
Call *Many Leagues Realty* and ask for Jules or Verne.

www.RealEstateThings.com

beached property

Close to Surf and Sand!

Port Between Storms . . . 180 degree ocean view, soon to be 360! Almost on the beach. Ask about our Outward Bound Mortgage Program. Hurry—this is a *liquidation sale!*

Dying to Settle Down? Your search is over! You'll never leave this home, graced as it is with finely chiseled, *marbleous* features everywhere. The CEO of Kelloggs-Post nearly bought it . . . until a home inspection revealed an infestation of cereal killers. Longterm tenants will stay. Quiet, dead end street. *Open House on Friday the 13th!*

Growth Opportunity!

Rare Commercial Property: Indoor nursery en root. Earthy decor with maximally flexible interior space. Massive skylight will cut lighting bills! Buy now and watch your investment grow!

The Last Straw

Almost Walking Distance to the Nearest Road! Reputed to have once been the summer home of the Thatchers, this cozy bungalow is the epitome of elegant simplicity. Decorated in neutral country tones, it exudes the unique charm of yesteryear. Exterior designed by Claude Monet.

eggstraordinary new listing

Eggstasy! This writing studio originally was built for famed eggsistentialist Sartre and the chick with whom he lived. It's truly all that it was cracked up to be! Call *Lovenest Realty*... and ask Henrietta for eggsact price and terms!

PHOTOS ©1989 BY SEAN DUGGAN

Country Estate! Howdy pardner. The Beverly Hillbillies' original homestead is now available! Special horsebarns (see page to the right) offer your family a uniquely *stable* home life. So don't stall . . . call!

Barnes Ennobled

tome sweet tome

Novel Forms of Housing!

This two story home is a classic example of *Multiple, Listing Books.*

www.RealEstateThings.com

tree house

PHOTO BY FRANK BLATTNER

Room To Grow! Trace deep ancestral roots . . . from the convenience of your very own *Family Tree*. Just step inside, into *Wonderland Realty*, and be sure to talk with Mr. Cheshire Katz.

PHOTO © JOHN ELK

Home Where the Buffalo Roam

To buy a-head of the herd... Just hoof on over to *Big Horn Realty.* Property includes free fertilizer and lawn mowers!

www.RealEstateThings.com

Has TWO (count them) Wood Burning Fire Places!

Indoor-Outdoor Beauty! Open-beam walls. Extra high ceilings. Features an unusual master bedroom sweet. Hurry or this stripped down model may soon be gone!

Toe Zone

PHOTO BY TAUFEK H. RAMSEY

If the Shoe Fits . . . tie up the deal! Designed for a straight-laced pastor who was really big into saving soles. This home's tongue-in-cheek features will wear quite well. Present tenant: an old woman with so many children.

upside potential

COVER HOME

Priced for Quick Turnover!

Great upside potential.
You'll flip over this one!

www.RealEstateThings.com

Starter Home for Insomniacs! (Not long or wide enough inside to lie down.) Interested? Then stop on by and leave a deposit. *Only a small amount of paperwork required.*

Star-Gazers' Castle! In this exquisite executive home along the shore, nearby waves will serenade you, while a special transparent roof is a bonus for amateur astronomers. The walls are so sturdy you'll soon take them for granite! The builders of this mansion left no turn unstoned, in their quest to provide you with that transcendental "Walled-den" feeling. To see this Thoreau-ly unbelievable home, call today.

truly private

City Solitude

PHOTO BY DMITRI KESSEL, LIFE MAGAZINE © 1990 TIME WARNER INC.

The Ultimate in Urban Detachment!

Here you can really *be* as isolated as you so often *feel*. Enjoy the conveniences of city living at its best, devoid of all those pesky neighbors you never wanted to meet anyway!

www.RealEstateThings.com

PHOTOS BY JENNIE CAMPBELL

De-vine Dwelling! Uniquely sited: location is easy to find yet hard to see. Wrapturous views from every bedroom. Completely captivating! Call *Land O' Giants Realty* and ask for Jack.

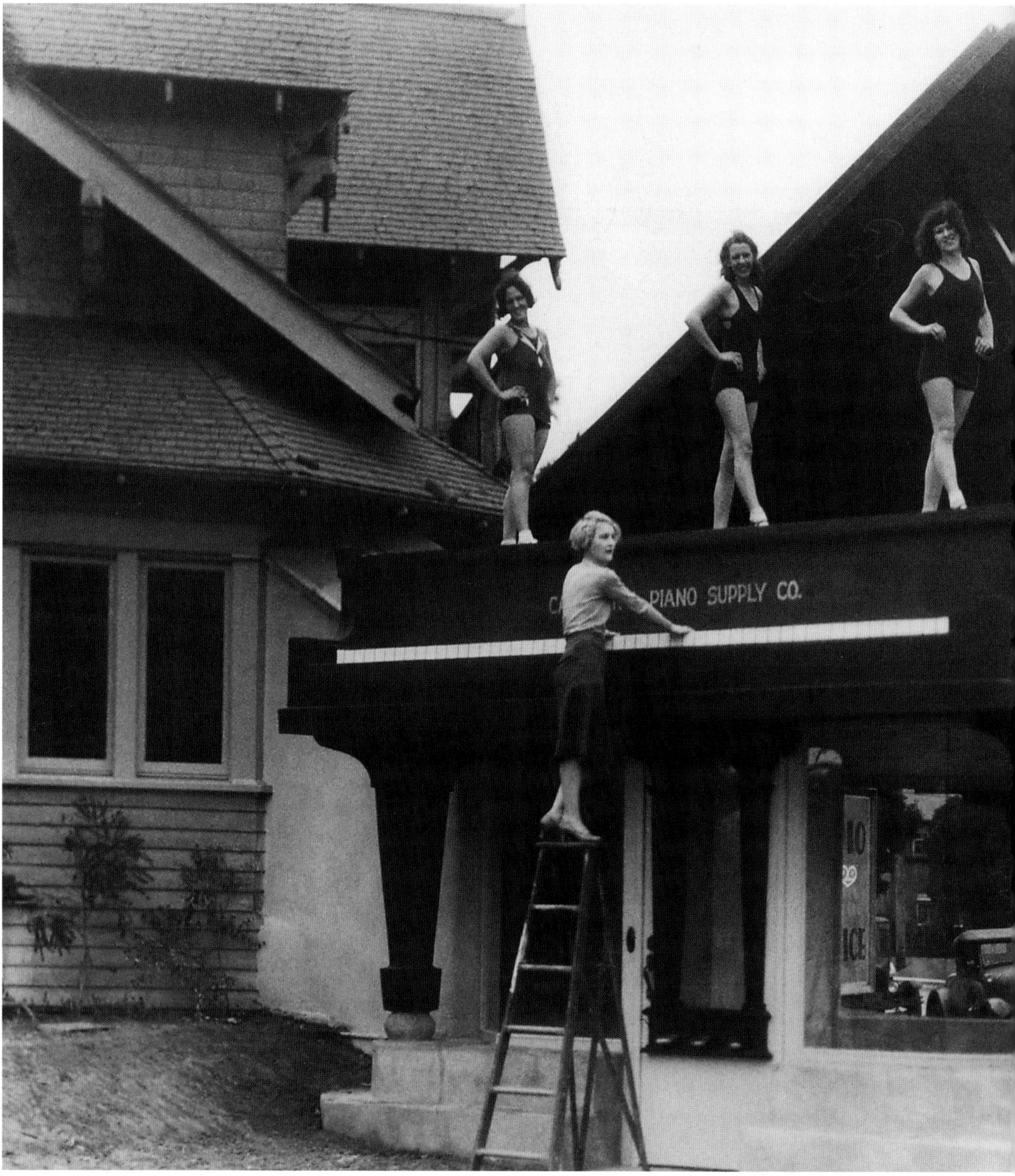
PIANO SUPPLY CO.

Play House! Find the right key and this dwelling is yours. Choose from four upright models. Call Mozart Realty and let Wolfgang or Amadeus be instrumental in composing a great deal for you!

Off-Street Parking!

PHOTO BY BILL LOVEJOY/SANTA CRUZ COUNTY SENTINEL

Friends Will Drop in to Visit . . . when you're conveniently located in this quiet refuge. A few days' handywork will return this charming home to a pristine condition. Safe location. Smashing view! So drive on over (others have).

Dynamic Views

PHOTO © 1982 BY PETER MARLOW/MAGNUM PHOTOS LTD.

Values Going up Quickly! Values are simply exploding in this bright and airy project. In these unusual new condos, you'll have a blast if you're single . . . and nuclear families will feel perfectly at home! Be the first to own a condo, here in the new Plutonium Gardens—a project that's just gone up! Call *Bit O' Heaven Realty* and ask for Peter or Paul.

PHOTO COURTESY OF TED ORLAND

Looking for a Branch Office?

Don't bark up the wrong tree. Instead, let *Forest Realty* show you how easy it is to increase your overhead. So well furnished you won't even need to pack that trunk. Original redwood interior—*Fido and Spot will appreciate the convenience!*

www.RealEstateThings.com

Real Potential

Handyman's Special! The pieces are all here—a great jigsaw puzzle project for the entire family. May not be around long, so buy now!

Catch of the Day! Home with a distinctive character. Unusual head room in the attic. Unique television antenna brings in all Cousteau series. *Don't let this be the one that got away!*

PHOTO © 1984 WILLIAM D. ADAMS

Sweet 'N Low! Owned by Mr. and Mrs. Peter Rabbit, these digs are currently on the *New York Times* "Best Cellar" list. To get into this below-market deal, call *Downside Realty,* a holey owned subsidiary.

Beach Get Away! Designed by a distinguished pole-ish architect, this contemporary home helps turn the tide on urban congestion. Originally built merely inches above what was once the beach, this home's value has been significantly enhanced by mother nature's own special landscaping system. Unique fire hydrant provides local canines with a challenge, thereby eliminating the elimination so commonly found at such sites. Local landscaping tax to be waved. *Offered by Tsunami Realty.*

champagne tastes, beer budget

A Good First Impression

Maintain a Great Facade!

Do you have champagne tastes but a beer budget? If so, this home will enable you to maintain the *appearance* of affluence, regardless of how little you *really* can afford.

www.RealEstateThings.com

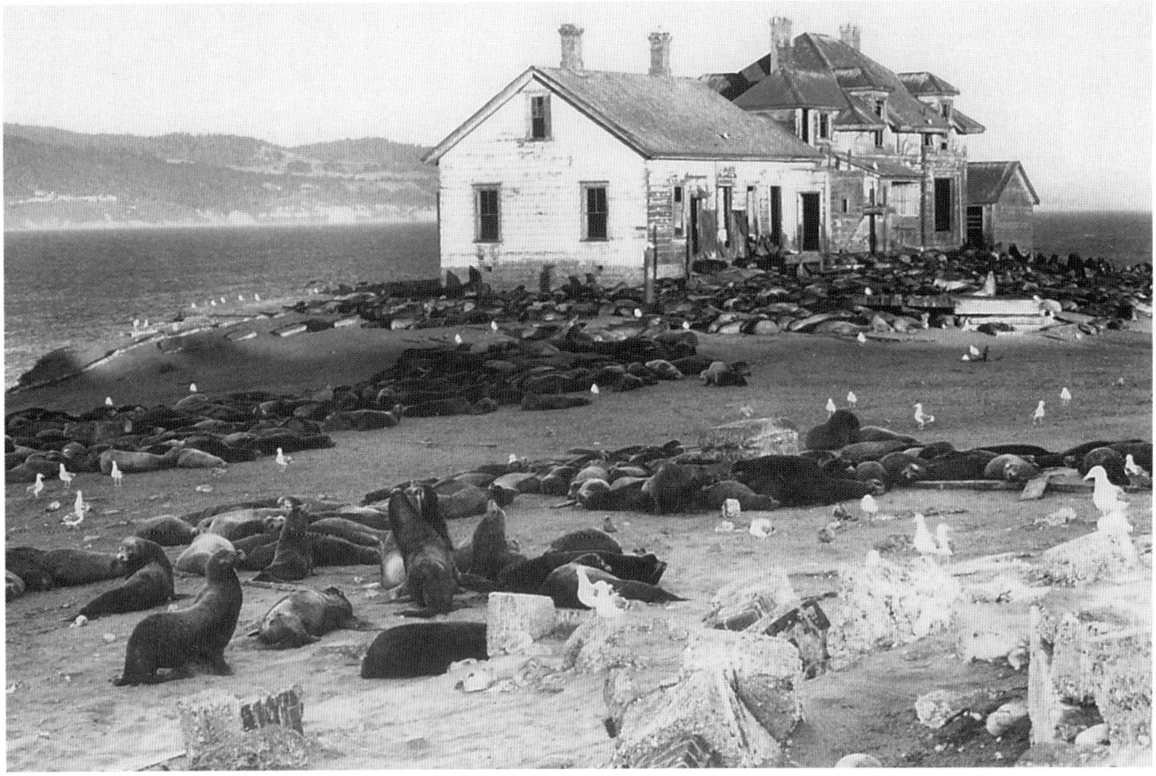

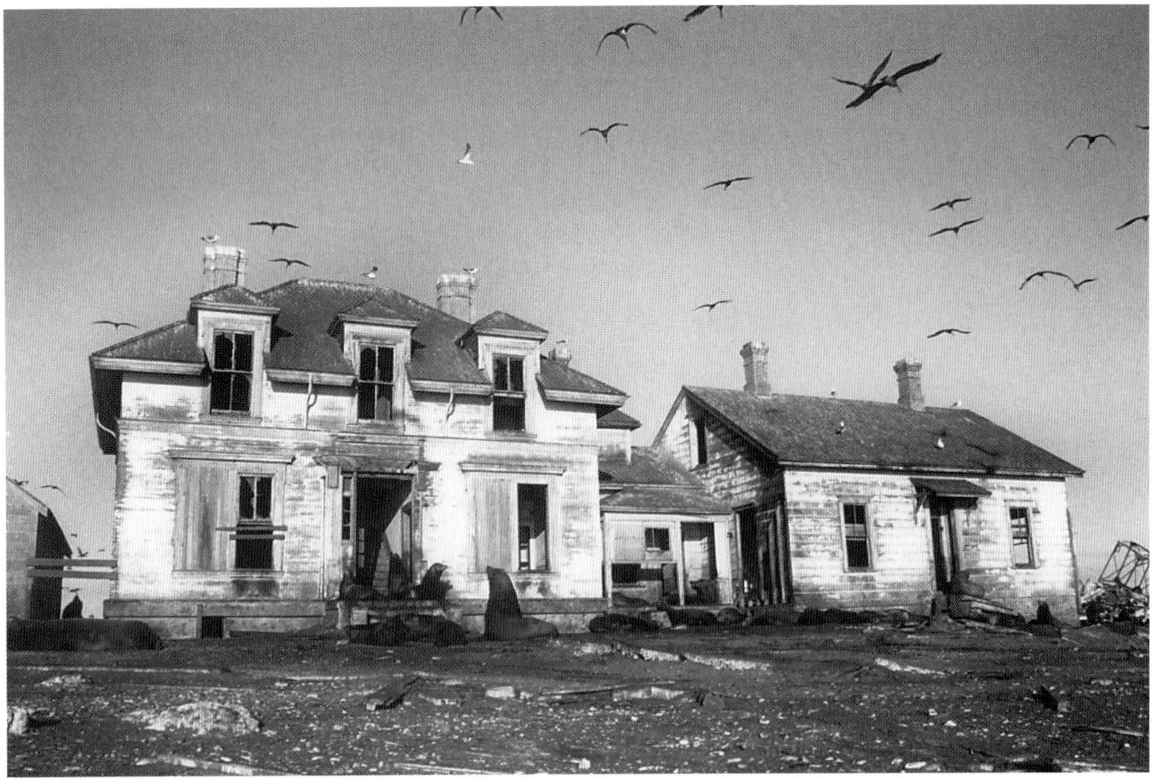

Good Housekeeping Seals of Approval!

This exquisite single family estate is brilliantly designed for in-laws or as an extended family compound.

Experience Lower Overhead . . .

here at *Crestfallen Condominiums* with . . .

Secure Parking for Compact Cars!

(Now that's *really* an under statement.)

PHOTOS BY SUSAN MCPHEE

This Place Rocks!
To enjoy life inside this "whale of a deal,"
Call *Moby Realty* and ask for Dick.

A River Ran Through It!
Oops.

Granite Counter Tops

A Boulder Design Approach!

Created by a famous Zen gardener, this kitchen offers solid design features at a rock bottom price!

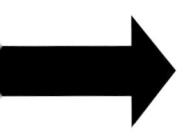

Only a Tiny Mortgage!

Architect's Model of a Soon-To-Be-Built Fixer-Upper . . .

Be the first to own a *brand new* fixer-upper! Choose your own carpets, colors, and drapes. Because it's Queen Anne-style, the rooms are a bit small. However, for a new home, this is the final word in Affordability!

PHOTO BY KEVIN COLE/BOSTON HERALD

House Mating? Tired of living alone . . . in a single, detached home? Looking for a house mate situation where you can share the very pinnacle of togetherness? Well, here it is! Mounting evidence proves that wrectangular construction like this promotes close encounters of the unforgettable kind.

www.RealEstateThings.com

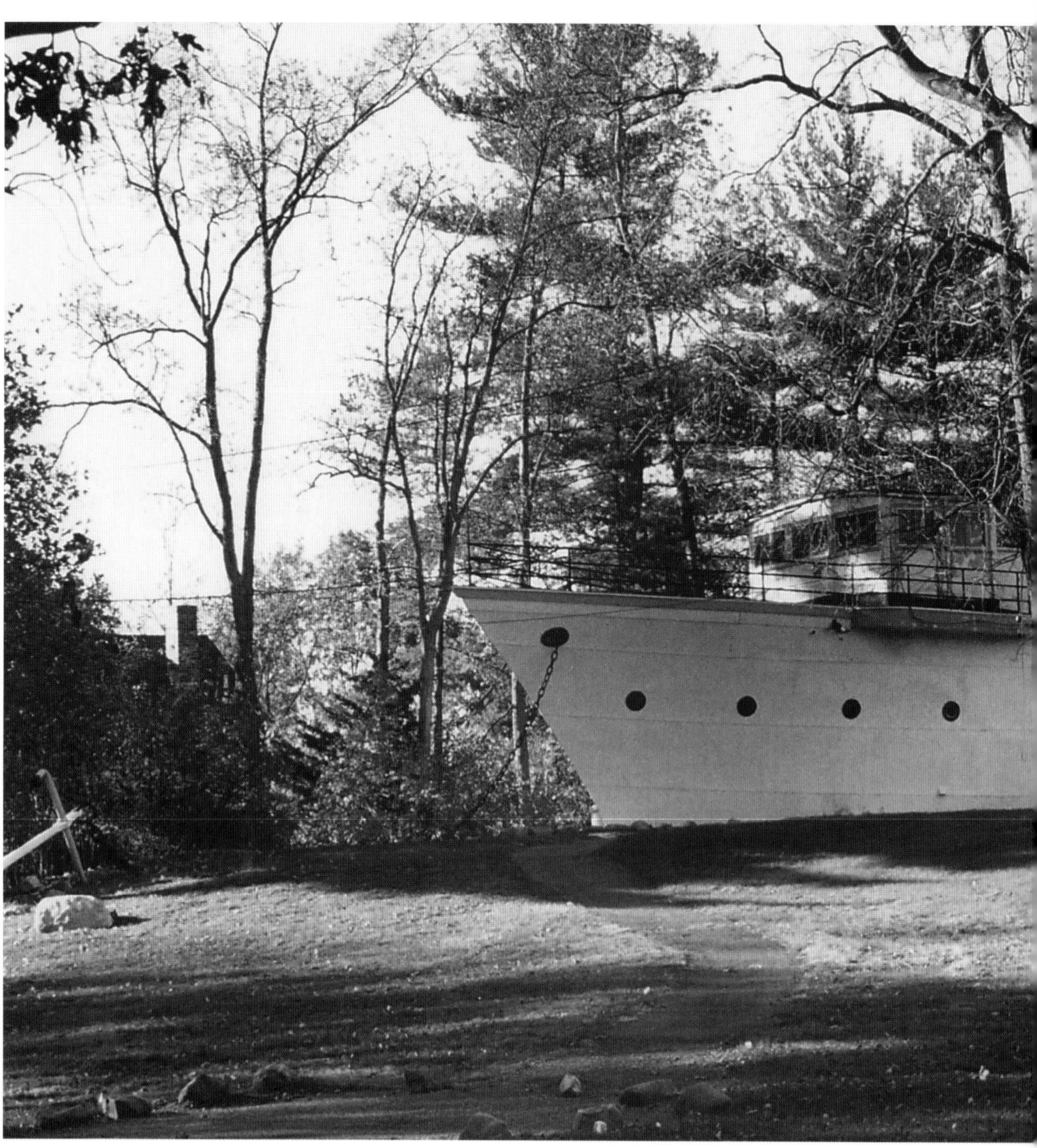

For Sail!
Totally ship-shape.
A *hull* of a deal!

PHOTO COURTESY OF JOHN BOSKO

Home for the Holidays!

Create Christmas presence every day in this ornamental beauty, while a "Sentry-21 Security System" guards against curious neighbors. Call *Santa's Realty* . . . and wrap this deal up before the holidays!

www.RealEstateThings.com

PHOTO BY JOHN BLONDIN/SEBRING NEWS INC.

Going ·····▶

PHOTO BY DAVID POLLER/ORLANDO SENTINEL

Going ·····▶

GONE!

Owner Willing to Float a Second! This home offers the ultimate in seclusion. It features underground utilities, covered parking, potential for a rooftop garden, private swimming hole, a step-down family room and an enormous wine cellar. *So grab this one quick . . . Seller wants out!*

downwardly mobile

Only Three-and-a-Half Seconds to Town!
Easy for sleep walkers to drop in on neighbors.
Perfect for the downwardly mobile!

PHOTO COURTESY OF FINE HOMEBUILDING

Establish New Roots! (and branch out in new directions.) Natural setting. Deciduous interior decor. Mature landscaping throughout. Bough House School of Design.

www.RealEstateThings.com

moving made easier

Tenants Now Vacating!

Please turn to the next page ➡

Just hanging around waiting for the moving truck . .

The next move is yours!

a real show place

COVELLO & COVELLO PHOTOGRAPHY

Open House! Exceptionally sunny eat-in kitchen. Unusual design makes it quite easy to meet your neighbors. A real "showplace." Stop by Sunday for coffee and donuts!

www.RealEstateThings.com

On the Nature of Realty

Residential real estate has been the symbol of "The American Dream" ever since the concept of overhead was invented. And real estate agents, who link people to homes and mortgages for durations that outlast most modern marriages, are indeed the high priests and priestesses whose sacred rituals culminate in the joyous state of home ownership.

Politicians and comedians (the former being a subset of the latter) like to address housing issues at every window, and likewise at every door, of opportunity. Why? Because such discussions hit home.

What does home symbolize for us? A safe haven, a fortress against the slings and arrows, the vicissitudes and exigencies of life. Whether one's home be a paleolithic cave under attack by herds of wild boars, or a three bedroom tract house surrounded by gaggles of human bores, our homes offer us tranquility, stability, protection and comfort.

Updated for political correctness, one might say: "A person's home is a person's castle." In brevis, our homes mean a lot (usually a very small one) to us, symbolically as well as practically. And that symbolism is part of what makes *Real Estate Bargains* so irresistible.

Jung (even when he was old) explained that homes are the external symbolic representation of our lives, bodies, and souls. This, he said, is apparent in our folk tales, dreams and daydreams. It's a good thing, I submit, that most of us do not need to pay rents, mortgages, or taxes on all of those properties we possess in our fantasies.

In his eminently readable book, *How Buildings Learn,* Stewart Brand says: "The whole idea of architecture is permanence. In wider use, the term 'architecture' always means 'unchanging deep structure.'" Brand continues, "Home is where you fall back into the self from the world, a place of honesty instead of aspiration, habit instead of ambitious striving. Returning to it you say with a sigh and double meaning: I'm home. (I've come home and I am home.)"

Architect Michael Benedikt, in his essay, *For an Architecture of Reality,* concurs: "We count upon our buildings to form the stable matrix of our lives, to protect us, to stand up to us, to give us addresses, and not to be made of mirrors."

Yet, upon occasion (perhaps as we peruse newly acquired facial lines while brushing our third molars), personal honesty and clarity prevail over wishful thinking. At such rare moments, we all are forced to acknowledge that, although we crave permanence, the only constant is change. That's as true of pay phones as it is of the creation, expansion, contraction and ultimate decline of domiciliar artifacts. And *Real Estate Bargains* is as much about what happens to buildings over time as it is about human whimsy.

For time itself is an artist, and a prolific one indeed. Using the tools at its disposal—such as rain, wind, dry rot, mildew, termites, earth upheavals and fire—time shapes and reshapes homes . . . and sometimes it even juxtaposes them with found objects and creatures. All is accomplished in ways that are at once both random and predictable. Clearly, I owe to Father Time, the ultimate sculptor, much of the material to be found in this portfolio of photographic wonders.

In a way, my work in *Real Estate Bargains* is aligned with Surrealism. Wallace Fowlie, critic of French literature, wrote of Surrealist art: ". . . the work, thus brought into being, is a mystery which can be felt and experienced without necessarily being comprehended." Surrealism, continues Fowlie, is a "way of reconciling man with the universe . . . it is a way of knowledge, of discovering the unity of the world. (Surrealistic art pieces are examples of) a communion with a peacefulness where opposites are united."

Mystery, puzzles, and strangeness have always piqued human curiosity. How often do we hear ourselves saying: What the heck is that?! What happened there?! How could that . . . Why, that must be a—huh?

Which of us is not inexplicably drawn to the mysteries of Stonehenge and Pompei? Who among us, when viewing a ruined castle, can resist imagining the royal pageantry, swirling dancers, and Arthurian passions enjoyed at those great mutton-and-mead galas of yesteryear? And why else were the most popular of nineteenth century Gothic novels invariably set in haunted houses?

In sum, we are attracted to the uncanny, as predictably as a moth is drawn to a candle flame; similarly, we are drawn to the whimsical, just as an ant is attracted to an uncle.

So, really, what is *Real Estate Bargains* about? Is it about residential real estate or is it about humor? About advertising or philosophy? About architecture or psychology? About something or about nothing? The answer to all of these questions is, of course, yes.

For me, the creation of *Real Estate Bargains* has been a fifteen year affair of fun and passion. I now can claim, with certainty, that you hold in your hands the most unusual collection of real estate images ever assembled. Moreover, all photographs are accompanied by what just might be the only examples of "lowku poetry" ever to have found their way into the realm of real estate advertising.

Do not delay. Enjoy every moment of *Real Estate Bargains* today! For the present moment is indeed our personal home in the plane of time—that fourth and perhaps the most significant of dimensions. ∎

References

Michael Benedikt, *For an Architecture of Reality*, ©1987, Lumen Books

Stewart Brand, *How Buildings Learn*, ©1994, Viking Press

Wallace Fowlie, *Surrealism*, ©1960, Indiana University Press

Humor and Profits

Humor generates laughter. It also generates revenues. Year after year, Budweiser, Eveready, Nike and Taco Bell spend megamillions to bring us funny ads; for, advertising built around humor has proven to be highly profitable. Similarly, public speakers and salespeople leverage our love of humor, using jokes and funny stories to sell us ideas, services, and an infinite array of products. In the workplace, surveys have shown that "a good sense of humor" tops the wish lists of many employees, when asked what they seek in a boss. Finally, as a nation of laughter addicts, we collectively pay Jay Leno and Whoopi Goldberg whatever they demand ... just to keep us chuckling.

Apparently we humans crave laughter nearly as much as we do chocolate, and we need it (except as newlyweds) far more frequently than sex. Why? What's so darn seductive about humor?

Funny though it may seem, the essence of humor is well worth examining. For, while its value may not be taught in business schools, humor is used by Fortune 500 and many other companies to boost their profits. Let's take a moment to examine *why* humor is so effective in marketing. Then, by learning *how* to use humor to achieve corporate and personal success, you'll soon be laughing your way to the top of your industry.

Humor Captures Attention: According to consultant David B. Wolfe, writing for the Dow Jones' magazine *American Demographics,* "The number-one challenge in advertising today is breaking through the clutter, and humor is one of the best clutter-busting tools around ... Use humor to turn a plain vanilla product into a brand loaded with personality and attitude."

We Americans are overwhelmed with data. We're numbed by floods of faxes, "news", e-mail, ringing phones, and other carefully designed assaults upon our senses. In advertising, cutting through information overload—*that is, capturing our attention*—is a challenge of Olympian proportions. Newspapers use the proven recipe of front-page violence to grab us; movies add a pinch or two of sex to the mix.

But for the majority of product and service marketers, using sex or violence to attract attention is perilous, since both of them repel far too many potential customers. Most advertisers, then, are left with one and only one consistently reliable tactic for "cutting through the clutter"—other than relying solely upon the grace of God for marketing success. What? *Humor!* Well-crafted humor gets noticed. It provides a competitive edge. Without it, advertisers are much less likely to snag potential customers' attention sufficiently to differentiate themselves from the competition. That's why humor is *the top tool* for ad campaigns that succeed and endure. Remember: he who laughs last ... is the slowest thinker. Humor rules. Get with it.

> "A smile is the shortest distance between two people."
> —VICTOR BORGE

Humor Connects People by Communicating Good Will: "A smile is the shortest distance between two people," comedian Victor Borge has said. Another guy, Charles Darwin (the father of evolutionary theory), suggested that smiling is an inherited trait to which we're all naturally drawn, and humor is the number one trigger of shared smiles. *Those who use humor demonstrate an intention to please.* According to Darwin, the feelings conveyed are friendliness, safety, non-aggressiveness, and the willingness to "go the extra mile" in pleasing others. Using humor, then, cuts through the clutter of data overload, *while at the same time* it persuades people that you (and your products/services) are safe, warm, and openly available. Humor has proven itself to be "The Great Connector." *Those who use it in marketing and sales show that they're contemporary, "hip," "with it," and on the cutting edge.* Even IBM finally figured that one out, thereby entering the twentieth century of advertising ... just as it concluded.

The "Inside Story" on Humor: Humor has chemistry—*real chemistry*—going for it. Science has shown that laughter reduces emotional stress and muscular tension, lowers blood pressure, and increases oxygenization by causing us to breathe deeply. Moreover, laughter stimulates our pituitary glands to release endorphins and other natural painkillers.

True, there *are* some sourpusses around; we all know a few people for whom smiling is painful. The rest of us, though, seek pleasure. Why? Because it feels good!

So laughter, like chocolate and love, makes us feel warm and radiant. And guess what? We are attracted to, then bond to, then pursue the people and products that provide us with pleasure. It's no surprise, then, that an advertising campaign has a higher likelihood of success, when the product or service it promotes is associated with laughter and the euphoria that laughing generates.

Humor "Has Legs": Laughter travels. That is, people talk about humorous ads because it's a fun way to share and bond with one another. Just as jokes are passed around the Internet at lightning speed, funny ads are frequently chuckled over when friends get together: "Hey, did you see the new Toyota ad? It's cool! There's this guy who . . ." Such everyday conversations bring attention to the speakers, laughter to the listeners, and word-of-mouth marketing to your company. This in turn multiplies an ad's exposure and value while amplifying, through repetition, the advertising's effectiveness upon those who view it. Result: your company and what it offers are remembered . . . and remembered *favorably*. In an advertising campaign, then, clever and outstanding humor creates an upward spiral of exponentially growing good will.

Be Noticed, Be a Hero . . . and Be Remembered: To sum up, humor is powerful and profitable. Use it in your company's marketing materials to capture attention, communicate a desire to please customers, generate word-of-mouth publicity, and to be remembered with enthusiasm.

"You cannot bore people into buying your product," said David Ogilvy, the father of modern advertising. Rather, in today's world, a company *must interest people,* in order to capture both eyeballs and market share. So use humor—advertising's most powerful tool—to add fun, punch, and memorability to your marketing campaigns. Then sit back and watch your bottom line grow! ∎

PHOTO BY JOHN KAEMMERLING

Owner will carry . . .

Author Poriss demonstrates the amazing power of leverage in real estate.

Author Martin Poriss is a marketing strategist and humor consultant. To learn more about using humor to increase your profits, by engaging Poriss as a consultant or keynote speaker for your trade group or corporate meeting, e-mail the author at:

martin@RealEstateThings.com

Notes of Gratitude

I wish that words could convey my deep appreciation for those many individuals who have contributed to the creation of this book during the past fifteen years. First, it is a great pleasure to acknowledge the prodigious efforts and creative input of my editor, Douglas Weaver, and of Marilyn Yasmine Nadel, my layout and design consultant. For more than a decade, these dear friends and colleagues have aided and abetted my development of *Real Estate Bargains*.

Much credit is due to those men and women who assisted by identifying strange and wondrous sites and/or by contributing photographs.

A warm salute is owed to Connie DeNault, Jennifer Greene, and Irinel Petrescu, all of whom modeled with spirited humor, thus adding a piquant touch of (still) life to this collection of photographic images. I'm also indebted to those whose helpful suggestions over the years have made a significant difference—Guy Berry, Wendy Boxer, Marilyn Darling, Ron Hildebrand, Hank Leach, Jim Little, Tom Livingston, Apolonia Morrill, Jack and Sarah Nelson, Nick Strickland, Eugene Tsui, and Susan Vaughan-Bongiorno.

Great appreciation is due to the owners of those homes featured in this book . . . some for their willingness to allow humor to be found in what they'd experienced as tragic losses, others for their own comic whimsy. Were it not for these wonderful folks and their homes, this book could not have been created.

My thanks to Robert Farber, Scott Mutter, Ted Orland, Aernout Overbeeke, and Jerry Uelsmann—dedicated and innovative photographers all—whose many words of encouragement helped me to stay "focused" on the artistic aspects of *Real Estate Bargains*. I'm also thankful to Brian Goggin and Jamis MacNiven—Bay Area installation artists whose works I admire—for their lively interest and generous validation.

Michel Spitzer, consistently supportive since my days as a McGraw-Hill author, has been a beacon of light upon this long journey. And, I'm eternally grateful to Bob Shayne—the talent coordinator with whom I worked on NBC's *Tonight Show*—for his ongoing friendship and unbridled enthusiasm for *Real Estate Bargains*.

In the world of real estate, I wish to acknowledge the special efforts of Jerry Bennett, a director of the marketing department of the California Association of Realtors (CAR). Also, the assistance of Fidelity National Title Company's Pierre Beniston, Bonnie Sease, and Bob Sutter was invaluable. And, of course, I owe the very idea of *Real Estate Bargains* to such local and national real estate advertising magazines as *Homes & Land*, for having inspired this parody.

At Century Publishing Company, Inc., Randy Rolphe, Paul Watson, Craig Rogers and Debbie Zak have been terrific friends and colleagues throughout the pre-press and printing process.

In all reality, I must acknowledge the influence of the great Surrealist painter, René Magritte, upon my own artistic efforts. Like him, I've spent far too long staring at a rather large Apple®. (This book is, to some extent, an outcome of my having done so.) Moreover, one of Magritte's key themes is echoed, in *Real Estate Bargains*, both stridently and loudly. Dear reader, *This is not a peep*. Not even close! Instead, this represents a *clarion call*...at least for those who choose to make a note of it.

Much love to Al and Bea Sisk, for having provided me with many decades of artistic inspiration and to my son, David, just for being who he is. And finally, my heartfelt thanks to Gary Bond, Connie DeNault, Stephen Gomes and Emily Toback, without whose support and assistance this book would not be in your hands.

As a footnote, I wish to acknowledge my indebtedness to Stan Freberg, Bob Newhart, and especially to Steve Martin—three guys I've never met, but whose inestimable and wacky creations have helped warp my own.

—MARTIN PORISS

Credits

This page constitutes a continuation of the copyright page. Every effort has been made to contact copyright holders and protect their rights, to obtain all appropriate permissions, and to credit proper sources. If an error, omission or inappropriate usage is noted, please contact the publisher and a correction will be made in the next and in all subsequent printings and editions.*

The author is grateful for permission to use photographs from the following sources:

- Half-Title Page: Original Redwood Interior—photo courtesy of Ted Orland; Open Floor Plan—photo by Devin Scillian; Ocean Front Property—photo by Steve Heaslip/Cape Cod Times; Champagne, see "Maintain . . ." below
- Focus on This One—photo by the author; building designed for Chiat/Day by Frank Gehry
- New Roe House—photos by author. Building designed by Eugene Tsui
- Almost Walking Distance—photo courtesy of Avoncroft Museum of Buildings
- Play House—photo courtesy of the Security Pacific Collection/Los Angeles Public Library
- This Place Rocks—photo courtesy of the Associaçao dos Arquitectos Portugueses
- Maintain a Great Facade—photo by author. Permission to use courtesy of Universal Studios Hollywood. *Note: this "Burning House" is no longer an attraction featured at Universal Studios Hollywood.*
- Tenants . . . /Just Hanging/The Next—photos by author. Sculptural installation, entitled "Defenestration," by artist Brian Goggin
- Back Cover: Commuter's Dream—photo by Jim Gensheimer/San Jose Mercury News; Split-Level Home—photo by Bob Linneman/Valley Press

Throughout this book, all of the photographs not otherwise credited are ©1989, 2000 Martin Peter Poriss (aka Peter Martin).

Book concept, text, cover and book design by Martin Poriss. Editorial: Douglas Weaver; Art and layout consultant: Marilyn Yasmine Nadel; Black/white prints: Bay Photo Lab; Duotones, separations, printing and binding by Century Publishing Company, Inc.

*Contact the publisher, Best Gift Press, through www.RealEstateThings.com

- Every home featured in this book is real!
- No images have been digitally manipulated or otherwise altered!

Artistic Intent

Images and text collaborate as equal elements in Poriss' work. The author/photographer juxtaposes and unites the familiar with the quirky, in order to satirize real estate advertising in a consumer-oriented society. By using black and white photography, the author engages the power of abstraction while avoiding the parodic cliché of reflective realism. To enhance artistic tension, the author has arranged the images in a graduated series as well as in the form of a visual 3-part fugue. Artbook-quality paper, duotones, and printing "sharpen the edge" and provide an ironic contrast to the Surrealistic photos, which are "framed" and thus completed by the captions. Over the course of fifteen years, author Poriss shot nearly half of the photographs in *Real Estate Bargains* and located or commissioned the rest.

The author considers this book to be entirely autobiographical.

About the Author

NOTE

Things are seldom what they appear to be. Rather, they are what we make of them. Reality is composed of many subjective choices. By looking with new eyes, we can turn every "lemon into lemonade" and reframe each fixer-upper into a palace. May we observe what is so, but determine what will be.

When dealt a challenging hand, we usually can rearrange the cards or draw others that—while always having been there—we had chosen to overlook. In short, by enhancing our realities, we can expand our life options. We each create "The Box," so we each can think outside it.

Take a moment. Close your eyes and dream. For, just as "We are such stuff as dreams are made on," our dreams are such stuff upon which realities are made.

—AUTHOR

Based in the San Francisco Bay Area, author Martin Peter Poriss* is a business development consultant and a real estate broker. He also provides solutions-oriented personal coaching for Bay Area professionals who want to make major changes in their careers or personal lives.

A *magna cum laude* graduate of Harvard, where his fields of study were psychology and communications, Poriss' first career was that of the on-air "Consumer Reporter with the Light Touch." Always combining humor with useful information, Poriss appeared frequently on *The Tonight Show* with Johnny Carson and served as the first on-air consumer reporter for NBC's *Today* show. He is the author of *How to Live Cheap But Good*, a McGraw-Hill best seller and Book of the Month Club selection, and he wrote a widely syndicated newspaper column for the *Chicago Tribune—New York Daily News*.

Poriss is the primary photographer, as well as the author and designer, of *Real Estate Bargains*. He collected the photographs in this book for more than a decade and developed the captions and unique book design during that time.

An enthusiast and patron of the arts, Poriss plays classical piano in amateur chamber music groups and is an avid choral singer. He is active in the Harvard Club of San Francisco and the Harvard Club of the Silicon Valley.

To engage the author as a business development consultant, real estate broker, or as a personal coach, contact him at:

martin@RealEstateThings.com

Author Poriss in one of his appearances with Johnny Carson on The Tonight Show.

*aka Peter Martin

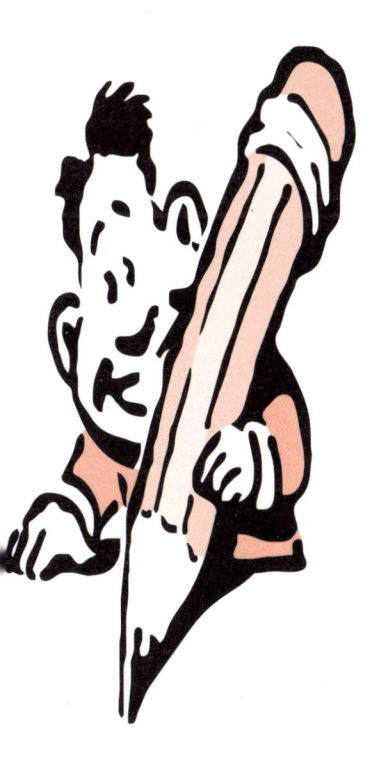

To order your Real Estate Bargains!
Please fill out one of the attached order forms or Call 1-800-824-1806
8:00 – 5:00 PST

Please send me _____ copies of *Real Estate Bargains!*
Single copies are **$19.95**, two or more copies are only **$17.95**.
Please include **$5.95** for shipping and handling for each copy. If you wish to pay by using your credit card, please call our operators at **1-800-824-1806**. If you wish to pay by either check or money order, please include payment with this card and mail to:

CENTURY PUBLISHING COMPANY
Attn: *Real Estate Bargains!*, Sales Department
P.O. Box 730
Coeur d'Alene, ID 83816

Please ship my copies to the following address:

Name: _____

Physical address: _____

Mailing address: _____

City, State, Zip: _____

Phone: (_____) _____

E-Mail address (Optional): _____

Note: Please allow up to 3 weeks for delivery

Please send me _____ copies of *Real Estate Bargains!*
Single copies are **$19.95**, two or more copies are only **$17.95**.
Please include **$5.95** for shipping and handling for each copy. If you wish to pay by using your credit card, please call our operators at **1-800-824-1806**. If you wish to pay by either check or money order, please include payment with this card and mail to:

CENTURY PUBLISHING COMPANY
Attn: *Real Estate Bargains!*, Sales Department
P.O. Box 730
Coeur d'Alene, ID 83816

Please ship my copies to the following address:

Name: _____

Physical address: _____

Mailing address: _____

City, State, Zip: _____

Phone: (_____) _____

E-Mail address (Optional): _____

Note: Please allow up to 3 weeks for delivery

Please send me _____ copies of *Real Estate Bargains!*
Single copies are **$19.95**, two or more copies are only **$17.95**.
Please include **$5.95** for shipping and handling for each copy. If you wish to pay by using your credit card, please call our operators at **1-800-824-1806**. If you wish to pay by either check or money order, please include payment with this card and mail to:

CENTURY PUBLISHING COMPANY
Attn: *Real Estate Bargains!*, Sales Department
P.O. Box 730
Coeur d'Alene, ID 83816

Please ship my copies to the following address:

Name: _____

Physical address: _____

Mailing address: _____

City, State, Zip: _____

Phone: (_____) _____

E-Mail address (Optional): _____

Note: Please allow up to 3 weeks for delivery

CENTURY PUBLISHING COMPANY
Attn: *Real Estate Bargains!*, Sales Department
P.O. Box 730
Coeur d'Alene, ID 83816

CENTURY PUBLISHING COMPANY
Attn: *Real Estate Bargains!*, Sales Department
P.O. Box 730
Coeur d'Alene, ID 83816

CENTURY PUBLISHING COMPANY
Attn: *Real Estate Bargains!*, Sales Department
P.O. Box 730
Coeur d'Alene, ID 83816